LETTERS
TO THE HEART

To Sandy,
A Great Coach +
constant inspiration!
God bless you.

Kim
Phil 3:10

LETTERS
TO THE HEART

How to Say the Things that Matter Most
to Those Who Mean the Most to You

Kim Beckham

iUniverse, Inc.
New York Lincoln Shanghai

Letters To The Heart
How to Say the Things that Matter Most to Those Who Mean the Most to You

iUniverse books may be ordered through booksellers or by contacting:

iUniverse
2021 Pine Lake Road, Suite 100
Lincoln, NE 68512
www.iuniverse.com
1-800-Authors (1-800-288-4677)

Because of the dynamic nature of the Internet, any Web addresses or links contained in this book may have changed since publication and may no longer be valid.

The views expressed in this work are solely those of the author and do not necessarily reflect the views of the publisher, and the publisher hereby disclaims any responsibility for them.

ISBN: 978-0-595-43055-0 (pbk)
ISBN: 978-0-595-87397-5 (ebk)

Printed in the United States of America

To Barbara, Jessica, and Amanda, whose beauty, wit, and grace inspired the letters that inspired this book.

Contents

Preface

My life has been about communication. For more than thirty years, I have tried to perfect the art of transferring ideas from my mind to the hearts of those who listen to me or read what I have written. The ability to communicate is one of the most important skill-sets we can acquire. A crucial part of communicating is connecting with those whom we value deeply in our lives. Many of us go through life trying to build homes and futures for our loved ones, yet we fail to clearly communicate to our spouse, children, and friends how deeply we love and cherish them. That's why I wrote this book.

Like many men of my generation, I was raised by a good father who, by his actions and dedication to providing for his family, showed that he clearly loved me. However, he almost never expressed that love in words and never in writing. Thankfully, toward the end of his life, he could tell me of his love for me and pride in my accomplishments, and I am grateful for those gifts. But I would have given anything to hear those sentiments when I was a young boy or in my teenage years, when I was filled with confusion and the struggles of growing up. I determined that my daughters would not suffer from the same uncertainty of love, and I began writing them letters early in their lives to express my delight and joy in their very existence. I learned that these letters became "treasured keepsakes" for my girls and that those simple words on paper helped me to build a deep and joyous relationship with both my daughters. It's a relationship that I still enjoy today, though they are now married women with families of their own.

As I began to share this idea with others, I received a powerful response, especially from men. So, I offer you this book as a primer to teach you how to write simple, yet powerful letters to those you love. I promise you this: you will impact their lives forever. Let's get started now writing "letters to the heart."

Chapter One

How to Say the Things That Matter Most to Those Who Mean the Most to You

"I hate my dad." I will never forget hearing one of my closest childhood friends say this of his father. He was angry because his father, as a busy pastor of a growing church, seemed to have time for every single person in the church but his son. One of the true tragedies of life is when we fail to connect with those we love the most. My buddy's dad was a good pastor of a fine church and a much-loved man in the community. I have no doubt that he loved his son, but he failed to communicate that love to him in a meaningful way. Unfortunately, this pastor is not alone. Far too many have failed in this critical relationship skill. As a pastor myself, I observed many times the hurt that occurred when a parent or husband failed to communicate their love. Early on, I decided I was not going to make that same mistake in my family. I determined that I was going to have a great relationship with my kids and my wife. Whether or not they knew of my deep love for them would not be left to chance or luck. I was going to tell them, and I did!

I began by telling them I loved them as often as I could, but I didn't stop there. I developed special, positive nicknames for them so that whenever I spoke them, they could hear the love. I called my youngest daughter, Amanda, by the pet name "What-a-Kid." I would say this to her at least once a week. "You know why I call you What-a-Kid, don't you? It's because you're a *what-a-kid* … I mean, *what a kid* you are, and I love you."

My nickname for my oldest daughter, Jessica, was "Wonder Girl," because when she was a preschooler, she was a fan of the television show *Wonder Woman*. I'd say to her, "Hello, Wonder Girl. I just *wonder* how I got to have such a *wonder*ful girl as you in my life."

This may seem corny, but it's a fun way to communicate your support and love. So many adults are still struggling to overcome hurtful nicknames that they were given in school or even, amazingly, by their own parents. I have heard awful labels like: "Skinny," "Fatty," "Wide One," "Slow Joe," and others given as nicknames. I have always wondered about the struggle these adults must have had as children trying to adjust to such painful names. Why not make sure your kids grow up with a special name that says, "I'm proud of you, and I love you?"

Did it work? Well, let me share a letter given to me on Father's Day this past year from one of my daughters, who is now a grown woman.

Dad,

There are so many things that I admire about you that I am not sure where to begin. I am extremely proud of you and all you have accomplished in your life. You have always been so driven and visionary. I know these qualities have allowed you to do so many different things in your life. You have never given our family a reason to be ashamed or embarrassed. You fight for our family when you feel we have been wronged. (I am sure this happens more than I probably know.)

You are supportive of my family, and your relationship with my children is amazing to watch. They love you so much, and their faces brighten at the very mention of your name. I know this happens because of the love and time that you have poured into them.

I also admire you for just being the dad that Amanda and I needed. You were always there for us. You supported us, and you loved us unconditionally. More importantly, you loved our mom and stayed with her, even in the hard times. You have given both Amanda and I such a perfect example of marriage.

Thank you for being the kind of dad that they write books about. I am honored and proud to call you my father. I love you more than I will probably ever show.

I love you,

Jessica

I have used many different techniques to communicate my love to my children and wife, but in this book, I want to talk about the most powerful technique I know for building self-esteem and strengthening your bond with your children and other loved ones. It's a simple skill that every one of us can use and that is guaranteed to impact your loved ones in an unforgettable way. I'm talking about letters, notes, and cards that come from your heart by way of your pen or computer.

David Dunn wrote: "There is something peculiarly *you* in the letter or note you write. It says, 'I think enough of you to sit down and try to put into words the interest I have in you.[1]'"

Letters have played an important role in human history. For instance, letters have:

- Taught us many of our most precious spiritual truths. The Bible includes twenty-one "epistles," or letters, ranging from the book of Romans to the letter to Jude.

- Started and ended wars. They have brought on assassinations and carried government pardons that have spared lives from execution.

- Sealed friendships and begun feuds that have lasted generations.

- Sparked romances and ended relationships altogether, i.e., "Dear John" missives.

- Been transported by human couriers, homing pigeons, telegraph wires, fax machines, and now, by electronic mail.

What an innovation it was the day humans began to write down their thoughts on parchment so that they could be transmitted accurately to another person, who might be miles and/or months away.

It's time for those of us who live in our busy worlds to recapture the tool of the letter to strengthen our marriages and inspire our children. I would love it if this book so motivates you that you are turned into a "letter-writing relationship-repairer."

Just think about the joy you feel on those rare days when you discover a personal letter or note buried in the pile of bills and junk mail that fills your mailbox. It's one of life's little pleasures to find a note from a friend—handwritten in their special script and addressed from far away. If such a surprise in your mailbox brings you joy, you can rest assured that it has the same effect on your own family and loved ones when they find a personal note from you amidst their mail.

Let me share a letter from my friend Lydia that came one day a few years ago:

January 27, 2003

Dear Pastor Beckham,

I just wanted to tell you how much I enjoyed the sermon last Sunday. At the beginning of the new year, it really gave me something to think about as far as my priorities and what "would I die for?" I'm looking forward to the next few Sundays and asking God to speak to my heart and reveal his will for me in 2003. Thanks for all your hard work. You are making a difference.

Sincerely,

Lydia

What a joy it was to receive this wonderful note on a busy day. I remember how much my emotions were lifted as I read this little note. It didn't cost Lydia much in time or money, but it made a real difference in my week.

Now that I've given you some examples of how letters can make an impact on those we love, let's talk about some of the advantages of using letters to communicate. First, you get the time to truly sort out what it is you want to say from all the jumbled thoughts of your mind. A letter gives you the opportunity to cull any unnecessary words or thoughts that would only confuse the issues you are trying to address. Second, the person receiving your letter has no choice but to digest your entire argument before they can respond, which is a huge advantage over a spoken conversation. Third, unlike conversation, you get a chance to rethink your words *before* you share them with a friend. E-mail is the exception to the rule here, because its technology allows letters in this format to be written and sent at almost the same moment in time. Be very careful with e-mail. I have a rule that whenever I write any e-mail that involves strong emotions, I must wait twenty-four hours before I send it. This rule has saved me from considerable embarrassment and emotional strife.

And the last advantage, but surely one of the most important, is this: if your letter or note is an expression of love, it immediately becomes a treasured keepsake, usually kept for the rest of your loved one's life.

When I was putting this book together, I asked my daughters if they had kept any of the letters I had sent them over the years and if they would let me copy them. To my surprise, they kept everything that I had written them. Even more surprising was that when I expressed the same desire to copy the letters I had written to my office staff, they, too, had kept every note and letter I had sent them.

Let's assume I have convinced you to begin writing the people who mean the most to you in life. Then, the next logical question would be: "To whom should you write?" Write to:

- Those you love.

- Those who are hurting.

- Those who may need to hear that they are important.

- Those whom we need to reach out to.

Here is a good example of reaching out to someone: I wrote a poem to my daughter, Jessica, one day after I had dropped her off at her school and realized that I had been so preoccupied with busy chores of the morning that I hadn't taken the time to really connect with her.

For Jessica, With Regret

I didn't tell you that I love you this morning.
I watched you walk away, and I was struck
By your beauty and courage, and my heart swelled ...
But I didn't tell you!

I was tired, and so I was grumpy.
I've been so busy and so strung-out.
I had my plans, my worries, my frustrations ...
And so I didn't tell you.

You were busy, and the morning's tasks called both of us.
You had things on your mind, and mine was swamped.
But there you were, beside me for a precious piece of time ...
Yet I didn't tell you.

I am sorry, and I want to tell you now.
I love you with emotion so strong that sometimes it tears at my
    heart.

You are one of God's greatest gifts to me,

And my pride in you is almost unlawful.
You are flesh of my flesh and the future of my dreams …
So I must tell you.

Please be gracious with a foolish daddy.
Please remember what I may sometimes forget to express.
Always know how much I love you.
Even when I forget to tell you.

Dad

By now, you may have decided that you want to write something to the important people in your life, but you may be wondering exactly what you should write. Here are some key thoughts to keep in mind:

- Write the truth.

  - A keepsake letter or note of encouragement is not the place for exaggerations or over-the-top embellishments. Simply tell the truth of your feelings for that person and how he or she has impacted your life.

- Open up your heart.

  - Don't let your note be only a superficial string of sentences filled with clichés and platitudes. Write down your love, pride, and joy in the knowing and being a part of that person's life. Remember, this is a letter from your heart! Don't be afraid to expose your tenderness.

I want to share with you a letter I received from my mother-in-law during my first year of marriage. She is, of course, very generous in her praise, and I'm sure I didn't merit all she wrote, but it is good example of writing from the heart.

April 26, 1974

To Kim,

About six months ago, I wanted to put my feelings about you down on paper, but somehow the words just wouldn't come. Today, as I was driving home, the words came easily.

As long as I can remember, it was always a joke between the two of us that you would take care of Barbara (like the time she fell off the horse). You were always such a sweet "brother" to her.

As I search my feelings, I think there was always a destiny for you and her. Barbara is a very special person, as you and I know. She talked with me several times about what she wanted to do with her life and the kind of man she wanted to marry. She set her goals high. You are the only person that I know of who met those qualifications. I am so proud of you for the stand you take for God. You have shown me several things that I didn't really understand, but as I listened to you (and I do), the answers came to me of some of the "whys" that I have struggled with.

As you continue your studies, I hope you won't ever look back but always press forward toward your goal. And I know that your goals are high. I will be 100% behind you, and if you ever need Pop and me, we will be there. How could we ever thank you enough for making our daughter Barbara so happy?

You will be celebrating your anniversary in a few days, and it reminds me of the Sunday after you were married. You came home early from your honeymoon to preach in the Sunday morning services, and the church was full that day. We were so proud of you standing there in the pulpit, but you said something that touched my heart. You said, "Friday night, I married the most beautiful girl in the world." For the first time, I realized we truly had a son.

To Our Son,

Momma and Pop Davis

By the way, I still have that original letter from thirty years ago in my desk. It is truly a treasured keepsake, as my mother-in-law was sharing her heart in a most open and powerful way.

Moving back to the ideas of how to write and who we should write to, I want to challenge you to be sure and write letters filled with encouragement when you write. Everyone has challenges in life, whether they are kids entering the first grade or senior citizens entering the "golden years" of retirement. Write to lift their spirits, to spur them on, to be their "pen-and-ink cheerleader." Your note could be the very thing that enables your loved one to keep on trying when they are ready to give up. Another area that is full of opportunities to write our loved ones is to share the lessons that God has taught us in life. All of us have had experiences that God used to shape our character and destiny, and they should be communicated.

To close this chapter, let me share with you a note I received after teaching this material at a men's seminar. I had just finished sharing with about two hundred men the concepts of *Letters to the Heart*, along with examples of letters I had written my children and wife. I always close my seminars on this subject by challenging the men to take time to write a note to someone before they leave the class. I even provide a sheet of paper with the first words written out for them that say, "There's something I've been meaning to tell you." One of the men present in the audience was a dear friend, who surprised me by giving me the note that I have included for you below. It is not only one of my treasured keepsakes, but it illustrates why you need to read the rest of this book.

Kim,

It is really interesting that your session would be about something that I have been doing of-late. Your teaching has underscored and put an exclamation point on this area. I have been composing letters in my brain for some time to my family and friends, but some of them have yet to make it to paper. Your session "pushed me" in the direction, and I will do this. I would also like to thank you for your friendship through the years and the wonderful example you have been as a father and pastor. May God continue to bless you and your wonderful wife. May the Lord bless your letters, and thanks for the much-needed encouragement.

Frank

In the chapters to come, I will give you practical advice on how to write effective letters and cards. I will guide you through the unique challenges involved in writing to young children, teenagers, spouses, and others we want to impact with our words of love and encouragement. My dream is that as you read the chapters to come, you will be emboldened to take-up pen or boot-up your computer and write something that will never be forgotten by those important to you. Let's get started.

Chapter Two

Saying the Most Important Things: Letters to Children

Most of us love our children and grandchildren with a passion that is beyond the imagination, but the question is, do the children in our lives know that we love them?

As Christian parents, we are commanded to train and encourage our children in their understanding of God and of life. Here are a couple of verses from the Bible on the subject:

> "Train up a child in the way he should go: and when he is old, he will not depart from it." (Proverbs 22:6, King James Version)

> "Fathers, do not exasperate your children; instead, bring them up in the training and instruction of the Lord." (Ephesians 6:4, New International Version)

I want to share with you a letter I received from my youngest daughter when she was just eight years old. She had wanted to go swimming at the YMCA, and I took off early one weekday afternoon to take her. I had also been reading her the classic children's book *Charlotte's Web*. This letter, as it appears in my keepsake file, is covered with hand-drawn pictures of hearts with arrows through them, spiderwebs, a bicycle, and a video movie-case. I have retained here Amanda's eight-year-old spelling and punctuation skills from those days, as I think it makes the letter even more precious.

Nov 11, 1989

Dear Dad,

I hope we get to read Crotles Web to night. I love You a lot. Thanks for taking me swiming Saturday. I really wanted to go. Maybe you can get me a new bike at Crismes this year. I alose want the move The Land Be For Time. Well I've got to go now but I still love you.

Love,

Your Darter,
Amanda B.

I am so grateful I took the time to take my daughter swimming on that long-forgotten day. I don't remember what was going on in my life at the time, but I know one thing: my daughter knew she was important to her dad, and something of lifelong consequence was built into her life on that winter afternoon.

We can't always take the time to take our children somewhere, but we can always find a few minutes to jot them a note or write them a letter expressing our love. Here are some age-specific pointers on how to effectively use written words to communicate our love to our children.

First, let's start with some of the problems connected with writing to our children. Most of these challenges center on the problems of age and social maturity. Of course, one of the necessities for writing to kids is that they must be able to read. What good is a letter to a toddler who has not even learned his or her alphabet yet? There is certainly some truth to this position, and we might want to use more practical ways to communicate to the youngest children in our lives, but let's not totally discount the idea of writing to our children, even when they cannot read. Wouldn't it be a wonderful gift to write a note or a card to your three-year-old that could be put up and saved until the child is old enough to read? Imagine the pleasure of a sixteen-year-old girl as she opens up an old yellowed and tattered—but deeply cherished—card that tells of her grandfather's delight in her when she was only three. Such a letter would be a treasured keepsake for any child.

Another challenge of writing to children is that they take whatever we say or write literally, with no understanding of metaphors or allusions. Children are extremely literal in their understanding of life and word. This is why we must be so very careful about criticisms when writing to the young. They have little capacity to measure the value of our judgments of their life and may be deeply wounded by our words. Just take it as a motto for your children that "criticisms can be deadly."

Remember that children have different stages of psychological development. A famous Swiss psychologist, Dr. Jean Piaget, has been teaching educators for years about the different levels of mental development in children. It was helpful to me to look at some of his categories of maturity, and I want to pass them along to you to assist you when you start writing to your children. Dr. Piaget identifies the following stages of the mental development of children:

1. Sensorimotor: Birth to 2 years

2. Preoperational: 2 years to 6 years

3. Concrete Operational: 6-11 years

    ("Reasoning ability is increasing rapidly, but reasoning is still quite weak. Learning is concrete. Children of this age reason in black and white."[2])

4. Formal Operation: 11-12 years to adult

This simple assessment leads us to think differently about writing to a first-grader than we would a child about to enter middle school. For instance, children in the first grade reason in an absolute and concrete way. If you say to one of them, "I am burned out," they will mentally picture you literally on fire, so you need to be careful about using sarcasm or adult clichés. Here are some examples of black-and-white reasoning from children in the wonderful little book *Children's Letters to God:*

Dear God,

Why is Sunday school on Sunday? I thought Sunday was supposed to be a day of rest.

-Tom L.

Dear God,

Is it true that my father won't get into Heaven if he uses his bowling words in the house?

-Anita

Dear God,

What does it mean you are a jealous God? I thought you had everything?

-Jane

Dear God,

Is Reverend Coe a friend of yours, or do you just know him through business?

-Donny

Dear God,

I wish that there wasn't no such thing of sin. I wish that there was not no such thing of war.

-Tim M., 9

Dear God,

If you watch in church on Sunday I will show you my new shoes.

-Mickey D.

Dear God,

I am doing the best I can.

-Frank[3]

I have a good friend who had the unfortunate experience of having a grade-school teacher ask him in frustrated anger, "Are you really that stupid?" That question was asked in front of his entire third-grade class and has followed him all of his life. As a man of sixty, he still gets tears in his eyes when he tells others of that experience. Criticism can be deadly with young children, so don't do it when you write to them. No doubt, instruction and criticism are necessary in raising children, but "letters to the heart" are not the right medium for this tool.

As we continue to think about what kinds of things we should write to our children, we can start by making sure we write and reassure them of our love and our personal commitment to them as parents. Mothers and fathers should put into words the deep emotions of affection that they have for their children—and get them down on paper. Then, these letters need to be placed into the hands and hearts of their kids.

To illustrate this concept, I want to share with you a letter I wrote to my daughter when she was just twelve years old. I had accepted a position as the pastor of a church, and that meant our family had to relocate to a new city. This change was particularly difficult on Jessica, as she was just entering middle school. Notice as you read this letter how I tried to reassure her and ease her fears.

Dear Jessica,

I want you to know that I am very proud of you. You are growing up into a beautiful young girl. I am so glad to see that your sweetness is growing, too. I like the way you are beginning to be able to say, "I love you," and hug us. I know it's not easy for you to share your feelings. You are truly a great kid.

I know right now is a scary time for you. I realize the idea of moving is frightening. I want you to know that I am a little scared myself. It is never easy to leave what you know to go to an unknown. I think about it a lot as I go about my work. I worry about how a move will affect you and Amanda and Mom. But, the bottom line is that I love God and have given him my life to use as he wants to. If he wants to move us, then I have no choice but to go. However, I trust him, for he has been my dearest friend, and I know that he will never hurt me or our family. Jessica, if God moves us, then even though it will be painful for awhile, it will be the best thing for us.

This time of indecision and fear has reminded me of how much I need all of you at home. You guys are the best thing in my life, and it's so good to come home to you after a "scary day" at work. No matter where we live or what we do, I'll always be there for you, Jessica. I love you and will take care of you.

When you were born, I saw you for the first time through the glass at the hospital. You were all red, and you were crying. You had beautiful black hair and looked so tiny and helpless. I looked at you and cried, and then I prayed. I said, "God, thank you for this precious girl. I will see to it that she never goes hungry, never is afraid, and never gets hurt." Well, I have learned that I can't keep you from every pain of life, and I am sorry for that. But I can be there for you to hang onto while it hurts. Hang onto me, Jessica, and I know it will be alright.

Love,

Dad

Children need concrete expressions of the love we feel for them. Why not take the time today to sit down and write your love for the children in your life?

What are some opportune times to write to your children? Times of problems and times of success are certainly prime seasons for sharing your love. Children need encouragement with problems they face in life. As adults, we often discount the emotional traumas of the very young, but everything is relative, and trauma is trauma. Children often have to deal with the death of a beloved grandparent, the moving away of dear friends, the stress of bullies at school, and much more. They need your encouragement. Write down your thoughts, and remind them that problems don't last forever, but they can be sure your love will.

And do not forget to seize the opportunities to write them and congratulate them on the successes of their lives. Medals won in gymnastic competitions, spelling bees, successful Little League teams—all deserve a card that expresses your pride and delight in their accomplishment. Making the ball team may seem like a small accomplishment to you, but in their short life, it could very well be their greatest victory. Celebrate with them in a form that they can save as a "keepsake for life." How do we write?

- Keep your cards or letters short.

- Keep your writing simple. Keep in mind the age of the child, and don't write the Great American Novel. Just share your heart.

- Make sure your notes are personal and not just clichés.

- Be as creative as you can. I am always amazed by the creativity of people. Here are a few creative ideas that people have shared with me about how they reach out to their children with written words:

I know a mother who told me that on many days when she made up the school lunches for her children, she inserted a short note to each child that expressed her love and pride in that child. She relayed to me that her kids told her when they got older, those notes tucked in the lunch boxes meant the world to them. She told me, "I'm so glad I took the time to jot down those little notes. When I picture my child opening up her lunch box on a difficult day and finding my expression of love, I know it was worth every effort I made to make that connection." She was right, and her kids love her like crazy. Another Mom shared that "it is very simple to make a paper banner to hang on the child's door or wall to surprise them when they get home from school." Imagine being a ten-year-old home from a rough day of school. When you enter your bedroom, you are confronted with a banner strung from wall to wall, saying, "what a kid," "you're the best fourth-grader in the world," etc.

The point is to get creative and find ways to write to your kids and anyone else who is important to you. Of course, some of you may be saying, "But you don't know my teenager." "How in the world can I write to her?" I'm glad you asked, because that's the topic of our next chapter.

Chapter Three

Letters to Teens

Teenagers are a different breed. Just when we think we have developed a close and loving relationship with our children, the change-agent of time slams into our homes in the form of the teenage years. Suddenly, everything is different about our children. A kid who was just a month ago an upbeat, active, fun-to-be-around youngster becomes a moody, angry, withdrawn teenager, who seems to cringe at the very thought of spending time with her parents. I joke about this with one of my daughters and say, "You were no trouble as a teenager. You simply went into your bedroom at fourteen and didn't come out until you were twenty!" That's, of course, an exaggeration, but not too big of one. We learned to be grateful for her self-imposed isolation as we spent time around other teenagers. No doubt about it, raising children successfully through the teen years is a job fraught with difficulty and emotional land mines. But here is where *Letters to the Heart* can be of great help to you. The teen years are almost made for maximizing the tool of the written word in strengthening relationships.

Let me share a letter I wrote to my daughter, Amanda, when she was thirteen years old and in the eighth grade. She was going through a trial, and the letter illustrates some of the key ideas to keep in mind when we are writing to teenagers.

Dearest Amanda,

I am writing to tell you that I love you and that I hate to see you as down as you were last night at dinner. I understand that a certain amount of depression is natural in teenagers, but I still hate to see you suffer.

I thought I would once more put into writing how proud I am of you. I think that you are the best eighth-grade daughter in the whole wide world. I love you with all of my heart, and there is little that I wouldn't do for you.

I want to encourage you about school. Sometimes things get off to a slow start, and it just takes a little time for things to come together. Just because the first two days of classes have been bad does not mean that they won't get better. You will make many new friends (who wouldn't want to be friends with a great kid like you?), and things will smooth out.

I also wanted to talk to you about depression. You may know that psychologists sometimes divide people into different personality types. One such listing gives four basic personality types: choleric, melancholy, sanguine, and phlegmatic. I believe that you fall into the melancholy division. Don't worry. This is not bad. You have much good company there. I am a melancholy, as have been most artists, writers, actors, painters, and geniuses. Melancholies have the ability to be creative and lift people up higher than they normally are. One weakness is that we tend to have bouts of depression. We are often perfectionists who think that everything has to be exactly perfect or we can't be happy. This can lead to much misery. I know that I have to remind myself that the world is not perfect and that I have to make sure I enjoy the good that is out there, instead of merely pining for what is missing. You will have to fight this tendency, too.

Remember that, although melancholies enjoy being miserable, no one else does. In this case, misery is not better when it is shared. When your friends make an effort to cheer you up, let them. Don't make them keep coming back to you time after time to convince you of their sincerity. This does not mean that you should not come to me or mom or anyone else when you have a problem. You certainly should, and we would love to help you. It just means that sometimes we have to face our problems and be happy anyway. Life is too short to spend it in depression. Remember, fake joy is better than genuine depression. Take the Bible's advice, and count your blessings when you feel down. Force yourself to smile. Sing a happy song, or listen to some upbeat music. Often, we can turn our moods around with some effort.

You are a beautiful girl who will be a marvelous woman someday. You have much to offer the world and much to look forward to. Try to enjoy your life as much as you can, and always remember that you can come to me for help any time you need it.

Love,

Dad

My daughter came up and hugged me after she read this letter. We had a wonderful discussion about life and its challenges as we reviewed some of its points. I am glad I took time to write it. She tells me that even years later, she still reads it from time to time for encouragement.

Let's talk about how to write to teenagers. Always praise the teenager before you attempt any kind of teaching or correcting. Even if you praise the child in the end of the note, if you don't start with praise, the young person may not read all the way to the end of the letter, and your praise will not have its desired effect. Don't be afraid of giving your child a "swelled head." Teenagers suffer so much insecurity that no amount of heartfelt and well-thought-out praise will be too much. It's also good to use metaphors and word pictures to make your points. Your teenager's mind is sophisticated enough to accept these literary concepts, and they can have a powerful impact on your ability to communicate.

You will definitely want to write of your own experiences and the wisdom you have gained in life. Use personal illustrations from your life that show how you solved problems similar to the ones they are facing as teenagers in today's society. When you use stories from your life, let yourself be vulnerable and open. It is much easier for your teen to connect with you when they can see that you had your own struggles with life and that you were just as fallible and human when you were a teenager as they are today. Always close your letters or notes with some of the positive expectations you have for their life. It is tremendously encouraging for a young person to be told by their parents: "I know you can do this," or "I have confidence in you." People have a tendency to live into our expectations of them, and this is especially true when we are dealing with teens.

What are some of the good times for writing to our teenagers? One of the best opportunities is during a problem time in the life of the child. We need to remember that the teen years are turbulent and chaotic, or at least they can feel that way to our kids. Look at this quote from a well-respected Christian psychology textbook:

> "At age 12, a son or daughter is still considered a child. Four years later, that son or daughter will become a young man or young woman with an adult body, reproductive ability and a desire for independence. These four years are probably the most difficult years of a person's life. The major adjustments that must be made in this period can be greatly facilitated by encouraging independent decision-making and spiritual maturity during the first twelve years of life. Of course, parental guidance and discipline are necessary until children are on their own at the age of 18."[4]

Kids between the ages of thirteen and eighteen are often called on to deal with some of the most powerful issues of life. Issues like depression, peer-group pressure, sex, the pressure of school, and realizing that life is often not fair are present in the day-to-day lives of our teenagers. Renowned psychologist Dr. Robert Havighurst wrote about the challenges that confront teenagers during their adolescence. He identified eight tasks facing teens. I list them for you here.

Tasks for the Teen to Master in Adolescence:

1. Development of more mature relationships with peers

2. Development of appropriate sex roles

3. Acceptance of personal physique

4. Development of emotional independence from adults

5. Preparation for marriage and family

6. Preparation for a career

7. Development of values and ethics that constitute an ideology or guide to actions

8. Development of socially responsible behavior[5]

Teens have a lot going on and a lot of pressure in their young lives. So why not write to encourage them while they struggle with problems? Your encouraging note could make all the difference as they face a problem.

Don't miss the opportunities that come your way to congratulate them, either. Praise them in writing for making the team, passing a difficult school course, or going on a church's mission trip. Whenever they do something good, celebrate it, and put it down on paper. Those notes of congratulations will not only encourage, but they will be grasped by your child—maybe for the rest of their life—as reminders of your love and support.

Another good reason for writing to our teens is that the adolescent years may be our greatest opportunity to influence our children through our words. This is because of two things that are more true of teenagers than any other age group. The first truth is that they are old enough to think philosophically—to think in the abstract; to "think about thinking," as one psychologist put it. For the first time in their lives, they are not merely reacting to life, but actually capable of making strong, reasoned choices about their behavior. The second truth is that they are still young enough to change their behavior. The old adage "you can't teach an old dog new tricks" is used to describe the difficulty of trying to correct long-established patterns in people's lives. Change comes much easier to the young. Teen-agers are young enough to completely reinvent themselves when they have the right motivation to do so. Wise parents and leaders must take advantage of this window of opportunity to influence young people, and *Letters to the Heart* can be a powerful tool of change to help your kids. Write to them whenever you feel them drifting away from you. Write to them when they are close, but make sure you write!

As we continue thinking about writing to adolescents, let's not forget to write to our older teens. As parents, we need to keep reaching out to make contact all through the lives of our children. Just because they are getting older doesn't mean it's time to quit. One place where the benefit of expressing our love and support to our kids will show up is when we have to let them go out into the world.

Every child is being raised to leave. If you are not parenting your child with the knowledge that they are eventually going to leave you and become independent of you, then you're probably doing it all wrong. God gives our children to us for a few years to train and develop them. Then it is the most natural thing in the world for them to leave the "nest." There is nothing stranger than seeing a physically healthy and mentally strong thirty-something-year-old man or woman still living with his or her par-ents. There are exceptions, of course, but generally, we are seeking to give our kids "wings to soar" and so, at some point, we must let them go.

Some of these "letting go" moments make excellent opportunities to write to our children. Such a time might be the first year of college, when a child is living in a dormitory or apartment away from home. This would be a fantastic opportunity to write and share your wisdom on how to cope with life as an adult.

I wrote my daughter a letter that I put in the form of a prayer and gave it to her on her last night at home as a teenager. I hope you can see within it some of the elements to include in your own letters to your kids.

Lord,

It's her last night at home. Even if she changes her mind and moves back home after a few weeks, it will still never be the same again. Our opportunity to mold her character and shape her for you has, for the most part, ended. She is a young woman now, and she is on her own. Help her to do what is right in the many decisions she will have to make, and help her to keep on loving and serving you when she has no one to answer to but herself.

I thank you, Lord, for the eighteen wonderful years that you allowed us to have her in our home. She has been a wonderful joy in our lives. We have often wondered how other parents have complained about how hard it was to raise their teenagers, because Jessica has always been so much fun to have around. Thank you, Lord, for a daughter who has made me proud in so many ways. She has always been a great example at church, even when we tried to reassure her that she didn't have to be. She has been a responsible student and has become a good worker who shows a true work ethic. I am very proud of how she looks and the pride that she has taken in her appearance. She is truly a "chip off of her mother's block" and a credit to her gender.

I pray, Lord, that you will now do for her what I no longer can. Please protect her for me. I know that you really have been taking care of her all along, but while she was here, at least I felt I could watch over her. Please keep her from the meanness in this world as much as she can be sheltered. Help her to use her good mind to be careful, and send your angels to watch over her at night. Remind her, Lord, that she is always our daughter and that she always has a home to go to when she needs it. Keep her humble enough to be able to ask for help if she needs it and wise enough not to get into foolish messes. Help her to know how special she is and how much she is loved, and therefore, she should never allow herself to be abused on any level.

I love you, Lord, for your gifts to me, and surely Jessica has been one of your greatest gifts of all. May you be with her as she makes this move, and may you keep her all the days of her life. Amen.

Love,

Dad

We all love our children, and our teenagers are precious to our hearts. Don't just clothe them, educate them, and train them, but make sure you bond with them on the deepest level possible. Make sure you say the most important things to the most important people—your teens—and put it in writing.

But it's not just the children and teenagers in our lives who need to read our "letters from the heart." In the next few chapters, we will look at some other important people to communicate with and the special skills needed to be effective when **we write them**.

Chapter Four

Writing to Your Mate

Someone once said that when you are under stress, you tend to ignore and quit servicing those relationships that you have taken for granted—those that don't scream for your attention. Two of the most commonly ignored are our marriage relationship and our relationship to God. These connections provide some of our greatest support, but because our wives or husbands and our God seem to be willing to wait on us to get our act together, we feel free to just brush away our responsibilities to them and focus on the "fires" of our lives. Yet, we ignore our mates and God at our own peril. If we stay aloof, distant, or preoccupied too long, we may do serious damage to our bond with them and find ourselves alone and lost in the world. This book is designed to deal with our relationships with the most important people in our lives. I'll leave it to your minister to deal with what happens if you ignore God, and I'll talk about our mates.

Many men have arrived at home to find their closet empty and a note pinned to their pillow from a wife who has had enough and walked out. Often, the man will say something like, "I didn't even know she was upset!" or, "How could she leave me? Doesn't she know I can't live without her?" Well, the whole point of this book is to make sure she knows how you feel about her, because many wives feel their husbands' emotional lives are a mystery they would desperately like to solve.

Let's begin by looking at some of the reasons why men and women leave their deepest expressions of love for their mate unsaid. The most obvious reason is that a man will take it for granted that his wife knows how he feels. I remember one rough-and-tough cowboy who was in a discussion, and the topic was telling our wives that we love them. The cowboy blurted out, "I told her that I loved her when I married her, and that should be enough. I haven't changed my mind, or I would tell her so." Such logic may seem solid to men, but it is really a recipe for emotional disaster. We don't tell our wives or husbands we love them out of necessity, but out of delight, and that is the truth that every woman instinctively understands. Saying "I love you" in a note or card should not be a burden—it should be a delight. Women feel that if we really love them, we will enjoy telling them so as much as we enjoy eating our favorite brand of ice cream. If you are doing what you love, it's not work, and if we love our mates, finding ways to tell them so should not feel like a task that has to be eliminated from our "to-do" list.

Another problem that arises in our love relationships with our mate is the toll that the little squabbles of a marriage can take on our communication patterns. Even couples who love each other with a real passion can find it hard to speak their heart after years of emotional sniping from the cutting remarks made during the inevitable marital spats. The Bible warns "to beware of the little foxes that spoil the vines." Every husband and wife needs to heed this advice when it comes to the tacky things we say to each other. A couple of years of put-downs and caustic remarks about your mate may make it very difficult to open up your heart to speak the things that matter most to the one who matters the most to you.

One final area needs to be addressed. Some people have experienced the heartache of having tried to share their deepest feelings, only to have been ridiculed or rejected by their mate. Let me give you a powerful warning. Never! Never! Never make fun of your mate in his or her attempt at sharing his or her deepest feelings with you. No matter how awkwardly they may state their love, no matter how comical their attempt to write their feelings, don't laugh or criticize. To do so is to teach your lover that their feelings are not safe to be shared. Years later, you may find yourself longing to hear some expression of love from a mate who seems emotionally distant to you. However, the root of the problem could be traced back to the embarrassment they received when you took lightly an earlier attempt they had made to share their love. Don't do it. Always respect the emotional courage it takes for your partner to open his or her heart and share their love for you.

When should we write to our mates? We have an endless list of possibilities. Let me give you just a few. Start by making sure you write a card of congratulations for any significant success they have attained. For instance, here is a card I received from my wife, Barbara, when I finished my Master's Degree in Counseling. The card showed a ladder reaching toward the heavens, and when I opened it, I saw these words:

Kim,

There is no way to tell you just how proud of you I am. "Stick-to-itiveness" is a trait I greatly admire in any person. The fact that you have "stuck-to-it" and earned your Master's Degree fills me with awe. So few people start out with this goal and ever make it. I am so proud of you, and I love you so much.

Barbara

This card is kept in my special drawer of remembrances, where I keep things that are precious to me. Whenever I need a burst of encouragement, all I have to do is read my wife's words of pride again, and I am ready to "take on the world." I am so glad she took the time to write down her feelings for me on my graduation. What success has your husband or wife accomplished that you could use as an occasion to share your love for them in a note or card?

The birth of a child is another time to take your pen in hand or sit down at your computer and pour out your pride. Every wife would love to receive a note of love after she has risked her very life to bring your son or daughter into the world, so why not write it? You can write to celebrate job promotions or successful business campaigns, and, of course, you must not forget to applaud spiritual victories in your spouse's life. One staple of letter-writing are those days everyone celebrates every year in our culture; for example: birthdays, anniversaries, Father's Day, and Mother's Day. One Father's Day, I received a touching card from my wife. The cover said, "With Love, to my Husband," and talked about being the fulfillment of her dreams. When you opened the card, it said, "Being married to you is the best thing that ever happened to me … I love you, and I'll always love being your wife." But the best parts were her handwritten lines: "This card says it all: you are the very best father and husband. I do love you so."

That card went right into my keepsake drawer. It meant the world to me to know that my wife thought I was a good husband and father, and I'm so glad she didn't leave it unsaid.

One year, on Mother's Day, I took out a sheet of paper and for days, I wrote down something I appreciated about my wife until Mother's Day arrived. Then I printed the list and gave it to her. It was a home run, and she has this tucked away in her special keepsake box. Here's a copy of it, so you can get an idea of why she loved it:

Barbara—What I Appreciate About You

For the last fourteen days, I have been writing down daily something I appreciate about you, in preparation for Mother's Day. Here's the list:

1. Being 100% consistent in your love for me

2. Your willingness to put yourself behind your kids' needs and wants

3. Your sweetness to me when I am grumpy

4. That you still look fantastic, even as a Grandma

5. The loving care you take of me when I'm sick

6. The fun you are on a date

7. The work ethic you constantly display … you're such a hard worker

8. The way you beautify my life with flowers

9. The way you wait lovingly for my return home

10. The love you have for all the members of our family, including the four-footed ones

11. The fun you are on our days off

12. Your steadiness and consistency … I lean on that every day of my life.

13. Your willingness to do what is uncomfortable for others (i.e.), speak in church

14. Your kindness to in-laws, my parents especially

Barbara … You were, and are, a great mom. You are a special treasure to us all.

Kim

Do you think your mate would enjoy getting a list like this? Why not start one today for that most important person? Regarding the kinds of things you should write to your spouse, I have four suggestions. But ... before I share them, let's look at this illuminating list from William Harley's wonderful book, *His Needs, Her Needs*, which details some of the most basic needs of husbands and wives.

For Men:

- Recreational Companionship

- An Attractive Spouse

- Domestic Support

- Admiration

  For Women:

- Affection

- Conversation

- Honesty and Openness

- Family Commitment[6]

This list of needs is as helpful to the letter-writer as a map of a strange land is to a tourist. It provides helpful and needed directions. Any man who wishes to score points with his wife will think about how he can speak openly and honestly about his affection for her and his commitment to their family. Also, any woman who wishes to endear herself to her mate will write of her admiration for him and her delight in their recreational outings, as well as praise him for his handsomeness and prowess as a lover. William Harley's list just confirms what I have often suspected about men and their wives, and that is: *what to write is not the problem. It's taking the time to write.* Let's get down to some specifics. I want to give you four reasons to write your mate.

First, you can write to clear up any communication problems in the relationship. Again, the wonderful tool of the written word shows its strength in enabling you to write your feelings, and the person receiving the information has to read the entire letter or note before they respond. It forces the person to be quiet long enough to really understand what the writer is saying before trying to respond.

It is an easy truth that men and women don't always communicate on the same wavelength. I saw a cute gag the other day, where someone had put together greeting cards for men in trouble with their wives and girl-friends. One of the funniest was the one that started out with, "I'm sorry for whatever it was I did." The rest of the card promised that "whatever it was" would never happen again—at least, he hoped not. This card is a wry expression of the difficulties men and women have in expressing their feelings clearly to each other. So get your pen out and start writing.

Men, how many of you have ever thought, "I wish I'd said I loved her," or "I wish I'd told her how I admire her courage," but you just couldn't dredge up the words during the conversation. So say it now. Get her a card, write down what you really wanted to say, and put it into her hands. Believe me, you'll be glad you did.

The second area we can write about to our mate is to make sure she or he knows how much we value her or him. It's one of the saddest tendencies of human nature to take for granted those who are the most reliable in our lives. We may cherish our mate with deep, heartfelt feelings, but if she hasn't heard us say so, it does our relationship little good. Everyone wants to be admired, and no one tires of hearing about their good traits. I have a friend who is truly gifted at making people feel special. Whenever he is around me, he always compliments my work, my family, or my clothing, and he is sincere in his praises. They are always well thought out and never meaningless flattery. Guess what? I'm always glad to see him. I can always find time to talk to this friend. I've noticed that he is this way with every-one, and everyone I know loves him. People love to hear of their good qualities. Why not take some time to list your mate's better qualities and drop them in the mail this week? Don't hand her the card, but send it by mail to work or the house. Let her have the joy of discovering it in the pile of junk mail and bills. I promise you, it will be a gift that will be remembered for a long time.

Another reason for writing to our mate is to open up our deepest feelings. Sometimes our relationships benefit from taking the time to really think through our feelings and trying to find a way to express our most profound emotions. Again, a letter forces you to really think about what you want to say. One of my heroes, Christian speaker and writer Fred Smith, advises, "When you have to communicate something important, write it down first." He says, "If you can't put it in writing, you don't really know what you want to say."[7] If that is so, and I think he's right, then the very act of trying to get your feelings for your mate down on paper will help you discover some new depth of what you feel for him or her.

One final reason to write to our mate is that it is just one more way to make her or him feel special. When people receive a card or a letter, it immediately tells them that you care enough about them to purchase a card or craft a letter, find a stamp, and visit the post office to mail it. These actions say, "You are special! You are important!" Why not write your mate today and confirm once again that he or she is the most important person in the world to you?

Here are some practical suggestions about how to write to our mates.

• Get creative.

  • Preprinted greeting cards can be a wonderful tool. Any Hallmark store has rows and rows of cards for every occasion that can help you communicate with your spouse. Try taking a photograph and enclosing it with your card or letter. With today's digital cameras and computers, you can easily snap a photo that will entertain your mate and will set your letter apart from the average.

• Get personal.

  • Remember, we are writing to the one we love here, so absolutely no writing in the third-person, please. Women do not want to read sentences like, "When *one* realizes that *one* is caring for *another*." That's awful. Write this instead: *"I realized today that I really care for you."* Keep it personal.

- Get risky.

  - Take a chance. Open up your heart and reveal more of who you really are. Tell them something they don't already know. Peel back another layer of your psyche and let them see the real you.

- Get "frisky."

  - Every once in a while, send your wife or husband a "for your eyes only" card. You'll start some fireworks for sure.

- Get clear about your devotion.

  - Always express your love and commitment. The point is to say the things that mean the most to the most important people in our lives. So always fill your letters with reassurances of your devotion and love.

A popular song says, "If you love her, find one hundred ways to let her know." I don't know if I know one hundred ways, but I know one terrific way. Write it down, put on paper, and say the most important things to the most important person in your life.

Now that you have a handle on writing to your soul mate, in the next chapter we will take a look at how to write to your adult children.

Chapter Five

Writing to Adult Children

No matter how old we get to be, we still like to hear praise. No one ever really gets past the point of wanting to say something like, "Look at me! Look what I can do." We all hunger for appreciation and praise. Our children don't stop needing our encouraging words just because they have left the home. The fact that they pay their own bills does not mean that they do not desire to hear your wisdom about life. After all, you haven't quit learning, have you? Then why should you quit sharing the lessons of your life with those you love most? Every stage of life brings its challenges, and as you work through each stage, why not write down some insights you learn to share with your children who are coming behind you?

I remember an old tale I heard long ago about this concept. A man was camped by the side of a powerful moving stream of water, when he noticed a traveler approaching the far bank of the river. He watched as the man carefully examined the flow of the water 'til he decided the optimum place to cross and then plunged into the tide. He saw how confidently the man moved, and in just moments, the traveler was up the bank to safety. Then he saw a strange thing. The man took an axe out of his pack and began to cut down a large tree. Out of curiosity, he approached the traveler and asked what he was doing.

"I am building a bridge across the stream," he replied, as he chopped vigorously at the tree.

"But why? You have already crossed the stream. Why build a bridge now?" he asked.

"It's not for me. You see, there is a young man coming behind me whom I have been watching, and this bridge is for him. I know that he is not an experienced traveler like me, and this stream might be too much for him, so I am building him a bridge." The observer walked away thinking how fortunate the young man would be to find this bridge waiting for him.

This is a great story. Why not take its wisdom to heart and begin to build some bridges for those coming behind you? Who knows the amount of heartache and pain you can spare your children by opening up your heart to communicate the lessons you have learned? We should continue to write our children throughout life. Let me share a letter I recently wrote to my daughter and her husband on hearing of a success they were experiencing in their work.

Hi Joel and Amanda,

Seeing you, Joel, at the church workers' meeting in Sachse yesterday just reminded me that I needed to get this letter out to you guys. As I watched you interact with the pastors and workers, and as I listened to them express their excitement over your evident success in Kilgore, I was filled with such pride. I probably can't get it down on paper just how proud I am of you both. I knew that you would have successful ministries, because not only are you both talented, you both have a deep love for the Lord.

I was a little saddened to see some other church reaping the benefits of your work and not getting to enjoy that blessing here at Central. I still believe it is best for you guys to prove yourselves in a church where your dad is not the pastor, but I sure do miss having your hearts and enthusiasm here with me. I guess that's just the price I have to pay for keeping our family out of squabbles.

But I am writing to tell you that no mom or dad could be prouder of their kids than Barbara and I are of you two. Joel, I believe your potential in the ministry is without limits, and I am sure someday I'll be getting introduced as Joel Byers' father-in-law. Keep on loving kids and loving God, and I know our Lord will bring your dreams to pass.

Amanda, you are no longer "What-a-Kid;" you are now "What-a-Woman." Your beauty is a joy to us all, and you have the ability to light up a room with your smile. I know your talents at graphic design will soon be showcased, and I am sure that your personal career will be long and fruitful. I love my Father's Day CD and look at it often.

Never forget that you come from love and constantly live in the deepest recesses of your parents' hearts.

I am so proud of you.

Love,

Dad

Wouldn't your son or daughter love to get a letter like this that affirms your love for them and your respect for their accomplishments?

The same concepts we discussed in earlier chapters will apply to what topics to write about to our adult children. Write to congratulate them on their victories and to share your wisdom, but most of all, continue to write them to share your love.

I have a friend who is in his early fifties, but even as an adult, he told me that he still thrills to hear his parents say they are proud of him. He shared with me an interaction with his family that I thought was revealing.

"I was sharing with my mother that I was working on a new project that would gain me some pretty wide recognition in my field, and the next week she told my sister about my new effort. I had occasion to call my sister about some matter, and we got to talking about my new project. My sister said, 'Mom is so excited that you shared your ideas for the assignment with her. She told me all about what you were doing.' I said, 'I'm glad she liked the ideas.' Then my sister said something else. She said, 'Well, I'm not sure which one of us kids is mom's favorite, but you are the one she is most proud of.'" He said that at that very moment, he made some kind of silly remark and brushed the comment off.

My friend then went on to say, "But here is the point about this comment—even if it's not true, and it probably isn't, because my mom is equally proud of all her children—I still was deeply moved to hear that my mother was proud of me. Now, I am over fifty years old. I have had a successful career and have earned my share of honors, but here I was being warmed to the very core of my being because of my mother's praise. I don't think I'm unusual."

We all want to hear that our parents are proud of us. That means your kids want to hear of your admiration for them. So get busy writing letters to them from your heart … letters that share your love and pride in them. I can promise you one thing. What you write will become a treasured keepsake more valuable than gold.

As an example of how to write to your grown children, I have included this letter that I wrote to my daughter Jessica and her husband on the eve of their marriage.

Dearest Jessica,

What an exciting time this is for all of us! Yours and Charley's marriage is not just the culmination of you guys' courtship, but it is also the fulfillment of many prayers your mother and I prayed over the last twenty-two years. Putting the wedding together is incredibly stressful, and I thought it might be good to write a letter to remind you of some important things and maybe distract you for a few minutes from all the busyness.

First, let me tell you again how much I love you and how incredibly proud I am of you. I think you have turned out to be a wonderful young woman, and I have high hopes for your life as a married lady, especially since I see you doing so many of the right things as you are starting out. You have inherited your mother's beauty and sweetness and maybe even improved on all her graces a little. I also want you to know that I completely approve of Charley and I am sure that he will make a fine son-in-law.

I know that you may be feeling some fear and sadness mixed in with all the joy of preparing for the wedding. No matter how exciting it is to enter a new life, everyone still hates to sever the ties with their previous life. It must hit hard when you realize that you are never again going to be the same little girl you have been up to now and that you are not just going across town to spend a few nights, but to actually set up a new life. Let me reassure you that you are always going to be our daughter and that you can always come home if necessary. Don't think of your life as a single girl ending, but rather just expanding to a married woman's life. I know that your mother and I do not feel as if we are losing you, but rather just gaining Charley and hopefully, someday, some grandkids.

Only foolish people enter into lifelong agreements without some anxiousness, but remember that you are a child of God and that he not only helped you decide to get married but has also promised to help you live out the vows you will soon be taking. Trust in the Lord and do your best, and you will be fine.

May I give you a few pointers that I think are indispensable to a happy marriage?

- Don't share your arguments with Charley with anyone who doesn't have to know. The fewer people involved in a battle, the better.

- Do strive never to go to bed angry, even if it means staying up all night.

- Don't let work or children or anything keep you from making time for each other every week. No romance can survive continual neglect.

- Do give God and the church first place in your home. God designed the home, and he will help keep it strong.

- Don't ever cheat on each other, no matter how tempted you are. Fidelity pays benefits that can never be replaced by patched-up promises.

Jessica Marie, I have loved you since the first time I saw you, and I will love you all of your life. You have brought great happiness to my life, and I look forward to many joyful days ahead watching your new family grow. Thank you for being a great kid, and just know that when I walk you down the aisle on Saturday, I will be bursting with pride and filled with thanksgiving to the Lord for letting me be your dad. Of course, I will also be crying inside and probably outside, too, but that will just be for a moment. I love you, "Jess-the-Mess," and I will miss having you around every day, but your mother and I raised you to "fly away" someday, and it's time for you to "soar." Never forget that you were conceived in love, raised with great joy, and are being sent out in pride.

I love you,

Dad

Jessica loved getting this letter, and she has kept it for more than seven years. Don't you think your daughter or son would also love such a letter from your heart? Why not take time today to write them something from your heart? Before I close this chapter, I want to enclose just one more example of writing to your grown-up children. This is a letter I sent to congratulate my daughter on her second wedding anniversary.

Dear Jessica and Charley,

Please forgive the formal look of this letter. I wanted to send you a card, but I have temporarily run out. I just wanted to congratulate you both on your second wedding anniversary. I am so very proud of you. A man couldn't ask for a better daughter and son-in-law. I am thankful for your work ethic and your financial wisdom and, most of all, your godly Christian character. So many folks my age are spending enormous amounts of time, energy, and money trying to help their kids who just never grew up. I am glad you guys have spared Barbara and me from that trauma.

It is also a joy to get to work with you in the church. It was not something we just counted on, as we wanted it to be you guys' decision, but I am so glad you chose Central. I am constantly seeing your involvement and the use of your talents for the Lord, and that is so rewarding.

Charley, thanks for being an even better son-in-law than we thought you would be (and we thought you'd be great!) It is a pure joy to see how happy you have made Jessica, and I appreciate the way you take care of her. Thanks also for sharing your skills in working with computers and construction work with us and thereby making possible projects that would have gone undone before you came into our family. I look forward to many years of enjoying your help and presence in our lives.

Jessica, as always, you are the greatest kid a dad could ask for. Do you remember running around the house in your Wonder Woman costume as a child? Well, I think you have grown to be a wondrous woman in every area of your life—in beauty, grace, skill, and joy.

Well, enough of this. I have a sermon to write.

I love you, and I am proud of your first two years. May you have many more to come.

Love,

Dad

Dads and Moms, try to imagine this scene. A harried young woman stops by her mailbox at the end of long and stressful day. Reaching into the box, she finds a hidden delight among the junk mail and bills. It is a personal letter from her father or her mother. She opens it, and tears come to her eyes as she reads of his or her pride and delight in her accomplishment after two years of marriage. She runs into the house to share it with her new husband, and, together, they re-read this note of love and appreciation. Can you imagine how much joy filled their hearts and how much stronger their bond will be with their father or mother? Why don't you write a letter to your grown children today? You'll be so glad you took the time to bless them.

Chapter Six

Letters of Legacy

My friend, Keith, has a special keepsake from his family. He has a gun cabinet that his grandfather, who is now deceased, built with his own hands. Keith loves this piece of furniture because of its connection with his much-loved grandfather. He says that every time he touches it, he thinks about what his grandfather meant to him and how much he loved him.

When we love someone, we desire something tangible that helps us connect to their memory when they have died. Letters from the heart can provide just that sort of feeling of attachment. The written word helps us say the most important things to the people who are most important to us.

I have spent my life as a minister of the gospel. One of my duties is to conduct funeral services. I cannot tell you how many times I have listened to a grief-stricken mourner say that they wished they could just hear their father say "I love you" again. Or even worse, they wished they could hear their father say "I love you" for the first time. When you write a letter to a son or daughter or mate and express your love for them, it will become not only a treasured keepsake, but also it will be part of the legacy you pass down to your family. What son would not love to have a handwritten note from his dad expressing his love and support to encourage him on the lonely days after his death? The "Dear Son or Daughter" letter is probably the most familiar form of what we have been discussing up to now in this book. We can all understand the powerful impact of a letter from beyond the grave, bringing peace and comfort to loved ones.

What should you write when trying to establish your legacy? A great example of this technique is found in the Bible. In the book of Deuteronomy, Moses leaves words of wisdom and encouragement to his successor, Joshua, who was like a son to him. Moses' statements to Joshua in this ancient book can serve as a template for you to follow in writing to your own children. What did Moses write? He wrote about the greatest victories of his life. He told, once again, of how God had helped him in the challenges he had faced, and how, through God's care and intervention, he had conquered all those who dared to attack him. Moses also wrote of the lessons he had learned from God and life. He recounted the turning-points in his life and went back over the truths he had discovered.

This is the very stuff that makes great letters. Tell your kids about your life. Tell them in writing about the times you were afraid, sick, angry, or filled with joy, and tell them why you felt that way. Tell them about how you learned to work hard, work smart, or just to keep on working. Tell them about how you fell in love and how that love made impressions that will never fade. Tell of your delight in being a parent and how you agonized over raising them. And, one more time … tell them how much you love them and how proud you are of them. Open your heart, and let them see the real you … the dad or mom that they loved, but maybe didn't know so well. I can promise you this. Such a letter will be a treasured keepsake for generations.

Here is a terrific example of a letter of legacy. It comes from Dr. Gordon McDonald and his terrific book *When Men Think Private Thoughts*. Notice how Dr. McDonald shares with his grandsons his thoughts and struggles:

> I'll still be reaching out to touch your grandmother and expressing myself to her in code words of affections that no one else can decipher. I expect to still be thinking of new ideas for books and sermons even when no one wants to read the books or hear the sermons. I'll be turning ideas over in my mind and relishing the good changes that are going on in this world. And if I have my legs and my mind, I'll still be wanting to work and make a difference in someone's life. That, after all, is my personal mission.

> I've enjoyed my life, Lucas and Ryan. Becoming a noble man through these years has been my greatest challenge. It's an elusive goal I'm still pursuing. Like the men I've described in this book, I have had many, many nights of private thought. Some of those thoughts I'd be embarrassed to share. But other private thoughts have taken me on to experiences of insight and achievement. On balance, I have only a few regrets and lots of delights.

> Finally, if you see me sitting quietly deep inside my private thoughts, please know that a lot of them are centered on the two of you. That you will be virtuous men, listening intently for the signal of God, serving your generation with vigor, bearing in your character the image of God. Go into the days of your manhood, Lucas and Ryan. Go with the knowledge that the men in your family line are proud of you, that we believe in you, that we love you. Go on with your dreams, and don't play dead for anyone. Be tender, gentle, strong, wise, and char-

acter-driven. In your private thoughts, be purposeful: in your public lives, be men of God.

And I say now what I told you I used to whisper in your ears when you were cuddling size: Papa loves you. That's among the best private thoughts a man can think.[8]

Isn't it wonderful to see how this grandfather so clearly expresses his love for his grandsons, and can you imagine how much his family treasures this document?

You can also write to clear up any lingering misunderstandings or quarrels. It's never too late to say "I'm sorry" or "I was wrong." And even if the fault is not yours, it's never a bad thing to reach out once more in love to seek reconciliation. It's funny how the things that seem to divide us magically disappear once someone becomes ill or near death. Do not take any chances on your children carrying a mistaken notion of some lack of love on your part in their hearts. Use the power of the written word to say the really important things while you still can.

Gary Smalley, in his excellent book *The Blessing*, gives five ways in which a parent can pass on a blessing to his or her children. They are:

- Meaningful touch

- A spoken message (Of course, for our discussion, we are implying using the written word.) Dr. Smalley says "silence leaves the child confused and guessing." When it comes to leaving a legacy, it's not enough to say "we were not critical;" we must provide positive comments of our pride and love.

- Attaching value to the one blessed

- Picturing a special future for the one blessed (I like the little lady who always referred to her son, even when he was just a little boy, as "my son, the lawyer!")

- An active commitment to fulfill the blessing[9]

Smalley's list has some great ideas to get your pen moving across the paper of your letter of legacy. Why not write it today? If you are shy and feel you would be embarrassed if they read your letter, put your letters in your will and have them delivered to your kids after you are gone. But ... write it down. I have one more idea for you in preparing this letter of legacy. If you just hate to write, then get a tape recorder and a blank cassette, and dictate your letter to your loved ones. Find yourself a private place. Turn on the recorder, and just start talking. A recording like this will be a joy and comfort to your family for years, if you fill it with your life and your love. Remember, now is not the time to be criticizing your family. This is an exercise in expressing your love and pride, so keep it positive when you are talking about them.

The key is to do it now. Don't wait until it's too late. Don't leave your family standing by your grave, wondering how you felt about them. Take the advice of the Nike shoe company, whose company motto is "Just do it!" You'll be glad you did, and your family will cherish its letter of legacy.

Chapter Seven

Writing to Employees

Every businessperson knows that once your business grows so large that you have to hire people to help you, then the level of your ultimate success will be determined by your employees or staff. If your staff is motivated and focused on success and customer service, you will see your company soar. Yet if they are undisciplined and lethargic and spend the day "watching the clock," then the finest business plan in the world will not save you from bankruptcy. The key to getting the most out of your people is motivation, and one of the most powerful motivators in the world is a handwritten note of encouragement. Think how good it felt for my secretary, Lydia, to find this note in her in-box one Monday morning.

Lydia,

Let me applaud you for the "Encouragement Ministry" you started. What an excellent idea! Your song Sunday lifted the entire church and personally affirmed my faith. Once again, you have set yourself apart as an exceptional worker and fellow servant of Christ.

Thank you,

Pastor

As a manager, I am not going to leave it to chance that one of my key employees feels appreciated, especially since it costs so little time and money to jot a note of approval and motivate your key personnel.

Here are some quick pointers on how you go about the task of writing to your staff. As with other forms of letters and notes we discussed, you want to make sure that your comments are specific to-task. For praise to be an effective motivational tool, it must be clear and succinct. We need to get beyond vague verbal "pats on the back" and give employees praise that shows we really understand the effort they put in and the actual work they accomplished.

Here is another example of a note I sent my secretary, Lydia:

Lydia,

Thank you for the excellent work you did on the CBC awards. As always, your attention to detail made us look good! More importantly, your efforts made us look professional. I appreciate you so much.

Pastor

Another idea to keep in mind when you are trying to encourage your staff is to express your dependence upon them—like this quick note I sent to one our employees, Beverly:

Beverly,

I would hate to try and do this work without you. You are a great worker and friend.

Pastor

It was short and sweet, but it was handwritten, and she knew it came from my heart.

Another great time to drop a note to your staff is when they are facing a challenge in their work. Employees who really make a difference are those who can step out of their comfort zones and tackle new tasks with confidence. But taking risks requires courage. When you have a boss who recognizes you are willing to "go out on a limb" for the company, it provides crucial energy for the task. Here is a note one of my supervisors wrote to me on the occasion of one of the first corporate speeches I ever delivered. It really "pumped me up" and helped me move on to the next challenge in my work.

Dear Kim,

I have not told you how dearly I think about you, and how much I respect your attitude, your involvement, and your character. Through you and your family I have been blessed again and again. God uses you in so many ways to bless children. I know your presentation here in Tulsa will plant lots of seeds of encouragement throughout the States.

God bless you,

Bill

I was grateful to get this card, and I keep it in my "encouragement drawer" in my office. It only took Bill a minute to write this note, but it kept me motivated for months.

Let me share one more way I have found to use written words to motivate people. We use a simple prayer card at Central Baptist Church. Every week, we gather our staff to coordinate our schedules and communicate about the upcoming ministry event on our church calendar, but we always take time to pray. We pray for any of the people of our congregation who we know are hurting or facing challenges, and we pray for at least fifteen families from our church roll. When the meeting is over, the secretary sends out this simple card that says:

> "We, the staff, believe in the power of prayer! Today, we prayed and called out your name(s) specifically. We asked the Lord to meet your deepest needs as you allow His Holy Spirit to minister to you."

Every staff member signs their name to each card, and then we mail it. You would not believe the positive response we get from this simple little card.

Here is a response that came from one of our members after receiving a prayer card on a week when we called out her name in prayer:

> I am not sure you will ever know (in this life) how much these cards mean to me! I do pass them on to my husband and I love you all and thank God for you and I pray back for you! It is quite often that I know God is real and somebody must be praying for me and my family. Funny how that still surprises me after all that God has done for me. Your prayers are a gift to me.
>
> Sue

The important idea here is that with just a simple little postcard, we are able to encourage and motivate members of our congregation. It might not be appropriate in your corporate setting to send out a prayer card, but the idea of a card from management that says by its very appearance in the mail, "I know you are here, and I value you," is one that can make a real difference in your organization.

Do you manage people? Do you own a business with employees who represent you in the community? Why not get started today using the written word in the vital task of motivating your staff? I read somewhere that someone famous said the greatest need people have is appreciation. More highly valued than money or fame, people want to know that their efforts matter. Remember the simple maxim of motivation, "What gets rewarded gets repeated," and reward your people with notes of encouragement and praise. It takes little time and very little money, but it will pay big dividends in your business. Get started today.

Chapter Eight

Writing to Those Who Are Suffering

When it comes to letters to the heart, perhaps the greatest impact we can have is on those who are in pain. This world is full of suffering. Someone once told me as a young preacher, "Preach to the broken-hearted and you'll never lack an audience." He was absolutely right. After thirty years of leading churches, I have seen more pain and heartache than I care to think about. As a pastor, I have been privileged to walk with people during some of the most trying events of their lives. I have been present when a husband received word from the doctor that his wife's tumor was not benign as he had hoped, and that the wife he loved so dearly may be dying. I have been at the bedside of those who are slipping out of this world into eternity, and I have held the hands of the broken-hearted as they walked beside the casket of the beloved family members. I know about grief and loss. I know the pain of losing my own father, and I know the heartache of having to make the decision about removing him from life support. I know suffering, and I know the courage it takes to face up the darkest times of life.

Certainly one of the most powerful tools we have to encourage the hurting is the written word conveyed by letter, card, or e-mail. When my father died, I received more than seventy cards and notes expressing support and love from my friends and from my congregation. I can't tell you how much they encouraged me. As I read the beautiful verses of the pre-printed cards, I was surprised at how comforting some the lines on the cards were, but I was most moved by the handwritten scripts in the center of each card. Those flowing lines testified to my friends' love and forever won them a place in my heart.

You, too, can use a card or letter to help lift the spirits of those who are hurting. I want to share with you a couple of notes that a lady I know received when she was battling cancer. She shared with me that the letters that meant the most to her were the ones that included references from the Bible. Here are some of her insights:

"These are the scriptures that spoke to my heart the most during my battle with cancer:

- This is the one I claimed daily:

  Isaiah 41:10 (New King James Version) [10] Fear not, for I *am* with you; be not dismayed, for I *am* your God. I will strengthen you, Yes, I will help you, I will uphold you with My righteous right hand.

- Other verses that brought strength to me:

  Isaiah 40:31 (NKJV) [31] But those who wait on the LORD Shall renew *their* strength; They shall mount up with wings like eagles, They shall run and not be weary, They shall walk and not faint.

  Psalms 18:32 (NKJV) [32] *It is* God who arms me with strength, And makes my way perfect.

- This final scripture reminded me that God is using me and my suffering for GOOD reasons that I couldn't see at the time and I may never fully understand until I reach heaven.

  Romans 8:28 (NKJV) [28] And we know that all things work together for good to those who love God, to those who are called according to *His* purpose."

I hope you realize what valuable insight this lady is sharing with us about writing to those in pain. I hope you will use her short list as a reference for writing to someone you care about who is facing a trial today. Here are some more brief, but practical, points on writing to those who are suffering:

1. Always share your heart. This is no time to be coy or formal. People are hurting, and they want to know you care.

2. Don't worry about not knowing the right thing to say; in fact, it's best not to try to explain why you think they are suffering. Just let them know you love them.

3. Be careful about writing, "I know how you feel." Even if you have experienced the same trauma, everyone reacts differently, and some people take offense at this remark.

4. It is okay to share something from your own experience, if you have been through a serious trauma, as long as you are just reporting what helped you and are not being "preachy."

5. Do feel free to include scripture references, if they are pertinent to the situation and faith is important to you.

6. Do let them know you are praying for them, if prayer is a part of your life.

7. Do send the cards or letters as quickly as you can after you hear of the loss or the tragedy.

8. Do send a follow-up note a couple months after the funeral has occurred. The long-term care for those in grief is often neglected. By six weeks after the funeral, most of the well-wishers will have moved on with their lives, and your friend may just be beginning to cope with the trauma of his or her loss.

Let me share another example of writing to those who are in distress. This note was given to me by a friend who was agonizing over the death of a father. Her pain was aggravated by the sad reality that her father was far from being the kind of dad all of us need. She gave me this note and told me that it was one of the most helpful she received during her grieving process. As you read her cherished letter from a friend, notice how her friend shares her heart and how wisely she respects the unique suffering of her friend.

Dear—,

Just wanted to drop you a line and let you know that my thoughts and prayers are with you not only now, but always. I was so sorry to hear about your dad. My heart breaks, because I try to put myself in your shoes and can only imagine how confused your feelings must be. The Lord says to love and honor our parents; however, in our case that's hard, since our parents didn't love and honor us as they should have. We still respect that they are our parents and try to obey God's word, but struggle with our hearts that have been broken. I don't know how I will feel or how I will handle the situation when my mom or dad gets sick or passes away. I can only imagine it will be hard, and I will have comfort knowing that I have a friend like you to talk to if I need you. You are truly the best friend I have ever known. I love you and admire you, and I cherish our friendship. I am now and always will be here for you! Please let me know if you need anything.

Love,

—

We live in a world of hurting people. Most of the suffering people around us doubt that anyone really cares about them. Why not pick up your pen and, through your words, provide encouragement, lift up broken spirits, and express your love for someone in pain? A handwritten note or letter often becomes a "cherished keepsake," and that is never truer than when we are writing to those who are suffering. Whom do you know who has suffered a defeat or loss? Will you write them today?

Chapter Nine

One Last Try

For eight chapters, I have been challenging you to take pen in hand or sit down at your computer and write "letters from your heart." Now I want to make one last pitch to get you to make a focused effort at communicating the most important things you feel to the most important people in your life. Let me tell you about a boy named Bobby.

Bobby was one of those little boys who just had too much energy and too little self-control. He wore his parents out when he was a youngster with his stubbornness and impulsive behavior. He was a terror to his Sunday school teachers and a frustration to anyone who wanted him to sit still. Bobby was the kind of kid a popular comedian was referring to when he quipped about an obnoxious youngster, "That's the kind of child that helps you understand why some animals eat their young." Now that is harsh, and of course, it's an exaggeration. Bobby was not a bad kid, but he was hard to handle. Now let me tell my story. As pastor of our church, I always send a birthday card to all of our church members that I personally sign, and I always try to include some encouraging words or compliments. As I looked at Bobby's blank card before me, I was at a loss for something to write. Just as a whim, and maybe as a prompting from on-high, I wrote, "Happy birthday, Bobby. I think you're a terrific little boy," and I signed it "Pastor."

The next Sunday morning, as I made my way to the sanctuary for the morning worship service, I saw the birthday boy standing near the entrance of the building. When I came up to him, he suddenly blurted out some words that caught me off guard. He said, "Pastor, did you mean what you wrote in my birthday card about me being a terrific boy?" Sensing that this was one of those rare moments we are given to make an impact on the lives of others, I said, "I sure do, Bobby. You are a great kid!" and I patted him on the head. He grinned at me and said something like, "Cool," and then skipped off. I went on to the service and forgot about our encounter until the next Sunday morning, when I spotted Bobby in the same spot near the auditorium door. He reached up his hand to shake mine and said, "Hi, Pastor!" and then bounded off.

Here's the kicker: For the next year, every Sunday morning, come rain or shine, Bobby was always waiting for me in the same spot to say hello and shake my hand. I had made a friend and had an impact on a little boy, all because of a few simple words in a birthday card. His strong reaction to my simple praise caused me to wonder if anybody had ever bragged on him before. Only eternity will tell how much that small note meant to a struggling little boy, but I had obviously made a difference in his life.

Why don't you set out to change someone's life today? Pick up a pen, grab a sheet of paper, and start writing. Start with these words: "There's something I've been meaning to tell you," and then tell them, in ink and on a sheet of paper, something that will become a treasured keepsake they'll hold onto for the rest of their lives. Why not jot a note to some overlooked person in your circle of influence today? I wish you the best in life, and I pray you'll make the effort to make sure you communicate the most important things to the most important people in your life.

Endnotes

1. Dunn, *Try Giving Yourself Away,* Page 57

2. Piaget, *Six Psychological Studies,* Selected passages

3. Hample and Marshall, *Children's Letters to God,* New York

4. Meir and Minirith, *Introduction to Christian Psychology—Adolescent Development,* Page 204

5. Havighurst, *Human Development and Education,*

6. Harley, *His Needs, Her Needs,* Pages 12-13

7. Smith, *You and Your Network,* Page 113

8. McDonald, *When Men Think Private Thoughts,* Pages 245-246

9. Smalley, *The Blessing,* Pages 24-28

Bibliography

1. Dunn, David. *Try Giving Yourself Away.* Inglewood Cliffs, New Jersey: Prentice Hall, 1947

2. Hample, Stuart, and Marshall, Eric. *Children's Letters to God.* New York: Workman Publishing, 1991

3. Harley, William. *His Needs, Her Needs.* Grand Rapids Michigan: Fleming H. Revell, 1986

4. Havighurst, Dr. Robert. *Human Development and Education.* New York, David Mckay Publishers, 1972

5. McDonald, Dr. Gordon. *When Men Think Private Thoughts.* Nashville, Tennessee: Thomas Nelson Publishing, 1996

6. Meir, Paul, and Minirith, Frank. *Introduction to Christian Psychology—Adolescent Development.* Grand Rapids: Michigan: Baker Books, 1982

7. Piaget, Jean. *Six Psychological Studies.* New York: Random, 1967

8. Smalley, Gary. *The Blessing.* Nashville, Tennessee: Thomas Nelson Publishing, 1986

9. Smith, Fred. *You and Your Network,* Waco, Texas: Word Publishing, 1984

978-0-595-43055-0
0-595-43055-4

Printed in the United States
108996LV00003B/214-570/A

9 780595 430550